# MARTIAL

---

## SELECTED
## EPIGRAMS

# INDIANA UNIVERSITY GREEK AND LATIN CLASSICS

# MARTIAL

## SELECTED EPIGRAMS

TRANSLATED BY

### ROLFE HUMPHRIES

INTRODUCTION AND NOTES BY

### PALMER BOVIE

MCMLXIII

### INDIANA UNIVERSITY PRESS
BLOOMINGTON

# Contents

# MARCUS VALERIUS MARTIALIS

WHEN MARTIAL CAME TO ROME in his mid-twenties from his native Bilbilis in Spain, he undoubtedly expected to pursue a career such as that of rhetorician and teacher, or legal consultant and attorney, or administrative official in the government. His education and literary talents would have equipped him admirably for these conventional duties and routine responsibilities; the support of Spanish friends in the circles of Seneca and Lucan, and later Quintilian,[1] might have been expected to lead to an appointment that would have made Martial solvent and secure and stoically contented with life in the capital. But nothing of the sort happened; we hear nothing of him until some fifteen years later when he published his first book, the *Liber De Spectaculis*, or *Liber Spectaculorum*, a group of short topical poems celebrating the opening of the Coliseum in 80 A.D.

[1] Quintilian, after a sojourn in Rome, had returned to Spain, presumably well before Martial's arrival. He makes his "comeback" when brought to Rome by the emperor Galba in 68 A.D.

Apparently Martial preferred shifting for himself to seeking gainful employment or the normal recognition that would come from meshing with the machineries of government, schools, or law courts. As a reluctant free lance, finding no ready-made niche of the sort he wanted to occupy, he instead set about carving a statue of himself. As he chipped away at this image, polishing, dusting, smoothing, and shaping the verses that would embody his objectivity, Martial managed to win what most artists want most: popular interest, patronage, and recognition of individual identity. At the end of Nero's wild reign and during the dark, exciting, and dangerous days of the Flavian dynasty, especially the era of Domitian, who in fact was one of his skinflint patrons, Martial took the measure of Rome in his own person and flourished in his proficient art.

If we evaluate his career in terms of his artistic production, we find him producing epigrams at the rate of about a book a year between 86 and 98 A.D. These formal publications were preceded by the "Book of the Games" and two sets of verse sentiments, the *Xenia* and the *Apophoreta* (comprising Books XIII and XIV of the *Epigrams*), cameo-like poetic tags meant to accompany presents. The presents which the *Apophoreta* describe are grouped in pairs, expensive and less expensive, and headed by titles, so that, as Martial says, the reader can stick to the label and not bother to read the whole couplet if he is in a hurry. These three sets of trivial verse identified Martial's style and, whetting the public appetite for more of his wit, encouraged him to continue proliferating epigrams; the statement he inserted in Book I of the epigrams at the time of a later reissue, that he is known in the whole world—*toto notus in orbe Martialis*—ricochets gaily off this fact. He was in production as well as in demand, but to judge from the arrangements of the twelve substantial books of epigrams, and the prose prefaces to several of them, the book-a-year pace must be taken to include collections, revised editions, and reissues. Martial attests to his own commercial success:

> As often as you run across me, Lupercus, at once you say: "May I send a boy to get from you your book of epigrams? When I have read it I will at once return it." There is no call, Lupercus, to trouble your boy. It is a long way if he sets out for the Pear-tree, and I live up three flights of stairs, and high ones; you can look for what you want nearer. Of course you often go down to the Potter's Field. There is a shop opposite Caesar's Forum with its door-posts from top to bottom bearing advertisements, so that you can in a moment read through the list of poets. Look for me in that quarter. No need to ask Atrectus (that is the name of the shopkeeper): out of the first or second pigeon-hole he will offer you Martial smoothed with pumice and smart with purple, for three shillings. "You're not worth it," you say? You are wise, Lupercus.
>
> I. cxvii[2]

[2] Quotations of prose translations of the *Epigrams* are taken from the Loeb edition of Martial; translations in verse are by Rolfe Humphries.

Some fifteen hundred poems and thirty-four years later, Martial left Rome in 98 and returned to Spain to live at leisure near Bilbilis, on a country estate provided for him by a sympathetic duenna in whom Roman sensibility combined with the openhearted generosity of a provincial grandee:

> Who would think, Marcella, that you were a burgess of iron-tempering Salo, who that you were born in my native land? So rare, so sweet is your quality! The Palatine will declare, should it but hear you once, that you are its own. . . . You bid my longing for the Queen City be allayed: you by yourself make a Rome for me!
>
> XII. xxi

A provincial, a city man, then finally a provincial again, Martial can compliment Marcella on her sophistication. He can also lord it over his friend Juvenal, stalled in the grinding business of daily life in Rome:

> Juvenal, while you're wandering around
> Bothered by the noisy stir of down-town,
> Or, perhaps, climbing uphill and sweating
> In some smarter residential section,
> While your toga flaps, or fans, around you,
> Think of me, after so many winters,
> Home again at Bilbilis, a farmer,
> In a town that boasts of gold and iron.
> Here I cultivate, with no great labor,
> Platea, Boterdum (our poor natives
> Name their villages with little music).

I sleep the clock around; I often idle
In my bed till halfway through the morning,
Making up for all the time I squandered
In my thirty years of active living.
Dress up? Never! I just have a servant
Sling me what I flung on a chair at bedtime.
When I do get up, the fire awaits me,
Heaped with splendid oak from the native wood-lot,
And my foreman's wife has breakfast ready.
I've a huntsman, too, a fine young fellow
You'd enjoy enjoying in the copses.
Look! My foreman gives the boys a hand-out
Telling them to go and get their hair cut—
(If they look like men, he can work them longer).
Country living, even country dining,
Juvenal, so help me, is the finest.

XII. xviii

Like Juvenal, Martial had learned not merely to sample
but to survive on metropolitan fare and to make the rounds:

In the first hour, and second, clients tire
Making their morning duty calls; the third
Sends the hoarse-voiced attorneys to the courts.
Till the fifth hour Rome tends her various tasks,
Then rests from sixth to seventh; oily wrestlers
Practice their holds and counters for an hour.
By then it's time to let our bodies rest
On soft-piled couches, and the tenth hour seems
The time to read my little book of poems.
Euphemus, when your courtesy has set
The ambrosial feast, and kindly Caesar soothes

His mood with heaven's nectar, his great hand
Around the half-full cup, that's time for jokes.
—My Muse has some reluctance about coming
To meet a solemn Jove at early morning.

IV. viii

Rome at least had the virtue of affording material for the writer and endless opportunities for nourishing his mind and exercising his judgment. Currying favor with "kindly Caesar" in the form of the blackguard Domitian was like ingratiating oneself with a cantankerous and lecherous Jove. But Martial did win some modest privileges[3] that made life in Rome easier for him. He enjoyed the benefits of some wealthy patrons whose largesse was real if disappointing. He lived in a garret for a good while: later on, he had a house in the same region, on the Quirinal, and a tiny house in the country nearby at Nomentum, both made available to him by Domitian:

I have, and by your grace I hope to keep,
Caesar, my dwellings in and out of town,
But the curved pole, bucket, and swinging sweep
Hardly suffice to wet my garden down.
My house complains that it is worse than dry
Though the great Marcian flume is rushing near:

[3] From Titus (and confirmed by Domitian), the privileged status called *ius trium liberorum*; by special grant from the Emperor this right could lead to preferment for a magistracy; from Domitian, the *tribunatus semestris*, an honorary tribunate carrying with it the rank of knight.

Grant water to my household gods, and I
Will think Jove's golden rain descended here.

IX. xviii

He is suggesting here that the town house be supplied with
running water from the famous aqueduct, the Aqua Marcia,
that goes by the house.

Martial was at home in interesting social circles; his
literary friends Juvenal, Quintilian, and Pliny were signifi-
cant, and he was familiar with most of the writers of his
day. His friendships were firmly built on affection and respect. The city never depressed Martial as it did Juvenal.
He found intellectual delight in the world capital and con-
veyed his sense of it in the finely fledged arrows of his epi-
grammatic verses, more often than not poison-tipped.

The social and intellectual atmosphere, if we may judge
from its reflection in the work of men like Tacitus and Juvenal, Pliny, Quintilian, and Martial, was very much like that
of London in the late seventeenth and early eighteenth centuries. It contained enough topical interest in its own para-
doxical realities to invite daily consideration. A reasonable
man might take the measure of phenomenal events and
ephemeral actors by plotting the average result of obvious
extremes: magnificent culture, power, and taste on the one
hand, and sordid deprivation and brute violence on the
other. There was room in the middle for the new writer
without status or security but with hopes for patronage and
commercial success.

> The Dean, if we believe Report,
> Was never ill receiv'd at Court:
> As for his Works in Verse and Prose,
> I own my self no Judge of those:
> Nor, can I tell what Criticks thought 'em;
> But, this I know, all People bought 'em;
> As with a moral View design'd
> To cure the Vices of Mankind:
> His Vein, ironically grave,
> Expos'd the Fool, and lash'd the knave:
> To steal a Hint was never known,
> But what he writ was all his own.

*Verses on the Death of Dr. Swift, D.S.P.D.*

Wit and satire, and deft adjustments to realities were required, not imagination and grand poetic designs. The artist could comment cleverly and forcefully on the scenes before him. There was no audience for one who might want to describe, embellish, and exalt; but every ear awaited the word of the gifted commentator. The great eighteenth-century voices sound much like their Roman counterparts, Swift like Juvenal, Pope more like Martial than Horace. Pliny is the very specimen of the eighteenth-century gentleman, country squire, friend of the great, a fine scholar with a secure prose style, who writes letters. Quintilian canonically discoursing on Roman literary history and style is like Dr. Johnson presiding over the English language. Even the languages have settled down, Latin into its "Silver" Age, English into its "Modern," no longer exciting and experimental but now clear and smooth and deadly. What the writer can do is to see what the world he writes in is like, profiting from being in it and revenging himself on it simultaneously. The sort of world which presents so many good subjects for satire can be paid back in the same coin, as Swift ironically records in the conversations of his survivors:

> Perhaps I may allow the Dean
> Had too much Satyr in his Vein;
> And seem'd determin'd not to starve it,
> Because no Age could more deserve it.
> Yet, malice never was his Aim;
> He lash'd the Vice but spared the Name.
> No individual could resent,
> Where Thousands equally were meant . . . .
> *Verses on the Death of Dr. Swift, D.S.P.D.*

The writer's strength in such an enlightened age stems from his frank and disenchanted appeal to reason. He leans on his solid faith in man's capacity to know and estimate himself. Instead of launching flights of fancy, he hands down verdicts.

Like his equivalent in eighteenth-century London, Martial in the epigrams is the ideal spectator, writing for a vast audience of spectators. If his first epigrams christen the Coliseum and are only as forceful as champagne frothing from the fragmented bottle smashed against the huge vessel it suddenly crowns, there is still a moment when the spectator is diverted from the spectacle. He is entertained, or struck, in quite another way by this symbolic blow, so that the event is an occasion for another kind of diversion. This subtle, reduced reality of impact is the key to Martial's art. The event is one thing, its inner excitement and meaning quite another; and people, no matter how far sunk in the slough of spectatorship, can be profitably entertained by being made suddenly attentive.

The epigram is one of the oldest literary forms and has rivaled the prayer, the ghost story, and the pun in longevity. As the term signifies, epigrams in Greek were at first "things written on" something, literary inscriptions like epitaphs and memorial verses, dedications, or sentiments put on gifts. In Greek literature epigrams distilled the lyric impulse to its tiniest tangible drop. Roman adoption of the device put epigrams to work as invective, sacrificing the flavor to the sting, or incorporated them into larger rhetorical patterns to climax a period, as Lucan did just before Martial, or Ovid did earlier in the *Metamorphoses*, and Catullus earlier still in many of his pointed lyrics. Catullus' most famous epigram is an elegiac couplet reading:

Odi et amo. Quare id faciam fortasse requiris.
Nescio, sed fieri sentio et excrucior.

I hate and I love. You may ask how that can be;
I don't know, but I know it happens to torture me.

Catullus 85

"It" seems to indicate the tendency of the Roman writer to switch the flow of his optimism and wholeheartedness into a channel of ill feeling. When Martial took up this verse implement, with its double aspect of being both a lyric and rhetorical device, he became its master. The style was certainly in vogue—Domitian erected so many triumphal arches and vaulted arcades in Rome that someone accused the emperor of being "arch" by the simple process of writing the Greek verb *arkei* (that's enough) on one of them[4]—and Martial traces his literary lineage back to Catullus through several writers of Caligula's reign. Petronius and Juvenal were in the air, and the invective turn of the epigram could buoy itself up handily on the thermal currents of satire.

Martial's own contention was that one epigram does not make a book, and the result is his total production of 1,561 short poems (that have weathered the centuries), the majority in elegiac meter with its inherent couplet rhythm, the others in various iambic rhythms or occasionally in hexameters. Sometimes he goes on at great length, often he is as brief as one could wish, but always his technique is such as to justify clearly his decision to move in on this miniature art form and worry it into shape for once and for all with savage aplomb. All later epigrammatists look back to Martial as their arbiter of taste. He influenced the epigram even more than it influenced him, and his successes set a high standard for future writers interested in this form.

The epigram is like the spectator with a ticket to the show; this little unit takes a sharp view of things. Its vision,

[4] Suetonius, *Domitian* 13, *arci* (the Latin transliteration of *arkei*).

focused in irreducible rhythm, neat shape, and clear edge
constitutes a judgment; and so in discussing epigrams we
seem justified not only in remarking upon their flavor but in
reviewing their verdicts. Martial is as personal and unique
as his epigrams; his opinions are as various and incon-
sistently provocative as the human behavior on which he
trains the mind's eye. Life is a jumble of spatial, identifi-
able experiences: the epigram proposes one witty toast after
another to life, and a prolific stream of epigrams becomes a
kind of poetry of experience whereby reality routs enchant-
ment.

Martial was so ambitious for his own books that he wrote
prose prefaces commending them to the good graces of the
dissolute Domitian, and epigrams praising the monarch. He
also flatters the Flavians by denouncing Nero—the memory
of whose physical presence in Rome the Coliseum was
intended to obliterate[5]—and his insincerity in this vein is
shown by his changing the tune accommodatingly for Nerva
and Trajan.[6] The poem for Trajan is particularly interesting because it indicts the false flatterers of Domitian, among
whom Martial was himself notorious. It does not result in

[5] *Liber Spectaculorum*, II: "Here . . . hatefully gleamed the
palace of a savage king and a single house. . . . Here was Nero's
private pond. . . . Rome has been restored to herself and under
thy governance Caesar [Titus], that is now the delight of a people
which once was a master's."

[6] E.g. X. lxxii (Trajan), XI. iv and v (Nerva).

the withdrawal of those earlier epigrams wherein we find the evidence to convict Martial on this count. I think this shows Martial's concern for the survival of his work[7] and an anxious claim for our attention to him as one who could write well on a bad subject.

Obscenity is another disenchanting feature of Martial's poetry. Martial proclaims that he will mince no words on the subject of sex, advises the relucant reader to skip the offensive parts, cites the precedent of such great lyric craftsmen as Catullus,[8] and goes right on casting these perils before our swains. Hearing from Martial about sexual conduct and misconduct is like attending a lecture given by a blasé Roman authority on the degeneracy of Roman

[7] Pliny's remarks bear on this point:
I have just heard of the death of poor Martial, which much concerns me. He was a man of an acute and lively genius, and his writings abound in both wit and satire, combined with equal candor. . . . But to say truth, what higher can be conferred on man than fame, and applause, and immortality? And though it should be granted, that his poems will not be immortal, still, no doubt, he composed them upon the contrary supposition.

*Letters,* III. 21

[8] "For the undisguised freedom of my expressions, that is to say the language of epigrams, I would apologize if mine were the example set: In this style writes Catullus . . . in this style every one who is read through. Yet if there be any man so pretentiously prudish that to his mind in no page is it permissible to speak plain Latin, he may content himself with the introductory epistle, or rather with the title." Epistle prefatory to *Epigrams* I.

morals during the first century, or like listening to Don Giovanni on love.[9] Whether the ingredient of obscenity strengthens or dilutes the whole situation of the epigrams, whether it is a concession to fashionable taste, or a shock treatment like bad news, or a social weapon like the scandalous episodes of satire "with a moral view designed / To cure the vices of mankind," each reader is free to determine according to his own standards of reason and experience. I think that the obscene epigrams, constituting after all only one-tenth of the whole product, are like a drunken friend, welcome and embarrassing. Any collection of Martial's epigrams that is meant to be representative of the man's work should not cold-shoulder this familiar souse.

Martial is not nice and easy-going, but neither is he merely vindictive and gross. In the group of epigrams

[9] Reviewing Don Juan's classical education, Byron asks:
> And then what proper person could be partial
> To all those nauseous epigrams of Martial?
>
> *Don Juan* Canto I, stanza xliii, ll. 343-4

Not to query whether "proper person" begs the question, we can offset "nauseous" by recalling Byron's own unheroic couplet later on in the poem:
> There's not a sea the passenger e'er pukes in,
> Turns up more dangerous breakers than the Euxine.
>
> *Don Juan* Canto V, stanza v, ll. 39-40

Handling the tragic figure with cosmic and comic irony, Byron is as clever and undeniable as Martial, and often epigrammatically wise:
> Though sages may pour out their wisdom's treasure,
> There is no sterner moralist than Pleasure.
>
> *Don Juan* Canto III, stanza lxv, ll. 519-20

nimbly marshalled by Rolfe Humphries from many poems, there is recreated the original variety of stroke and glittering steel edge. The poet is learned and self-conscious, and his skill is evidently a technical manipulation of neat forms, disciplined meters and the maneuvering of a few words into exact positions, where although light they carry weight. But Martial's art is also an art of meaning versed in experience, and his translator has achieved the same.

There is no room for the schoolroom—too noisy and pedantic, the education that teachers inflict is grossly unprofitable when compared with learning an instrument like the harp or lute. And let there never be summer school:

> aestate pueri si valent, satis discunt
>
> If boys keep well in summer, it's agreed,
> They're learning all the lessons that they need.
>
> X. lxii

The poet is impatient with mythology and "classical allusions," but he can apply them judiciously to the landscape obliterated by the eruption of Vesuvius, an outrageous blasphemy on the serene face of pagan natural beauty:

Here were the ridges that Bacchus loved more than the foothills
     of Nysa,
  Here on the mountainside Satyrs would leap in the dance;
Here was Venus' abode, a realm more dear than her Sparta,
  Here was the site of a town famous for Hercules' name.
Now it all lies choked and quenched under desolate ashes,
  Even the gods on high wish no such license were theirs.

IV. xliv

For nature's benefits Martial is genuinely grateful, and he sketches the landscape with an untrembling hand:

> More blessed than the gardens where
> The golden apples used to grow
> Are these few acres, looking down
> From their high ridge to hills below.
> This area, with its graceful swell,
> Enjoys a more untroubled height,
> And when the valley  fill with cloud
> Shines with its own peculiar light.
> How near the undiluted stars
> Beam on the graces of this home. . . .
>
> IV. xliv

Of course, his own scraggly holding at Nomentum is several cuts below his namesake's villa.

As for life, Martial voices anew what the experienced Epicurean might be expected to conclude. The healthy life is the true one: *non est vivere sed valere vita* (VI. lxx). Our days are infinitely precious and finitely numbered; the candid eulogy for graceful little Erotion, dead before her sixth birthday, is a variation on this theme in a minor key:

Fronto my father, to you and my mother Flacilla I tender
  This little serving-maid, joy and delight of my heart.
Don't let her shiver and shake in the shadowy blackness of Hades.
  Don't let her be afraid of the Hell-hound's horrible jaws.
She had arrived, almost, at one more of her few winter birthdays,
  She would have lived six years, given another six days.
Now let her romp as she will in the sight of her agèd protectors,
  Let her lisping voice utter the sound of my name.

Let the turf above her delicate bones lie gently;
  Rest on her lightly, O Earth, on whom her step was so light.

V. xxxiv

He helps make uncommonly memorable our common joys and sorrows.

Martial was better off in Rome than in Bilbilis because in Rome he found the villains and fools his art knew how to mock. In the metropolis, too, he discovered a host of readers and the two dozen good friends a man is usually entitled to have. When he went back to Bilbilis and dropped out of sight, it was as one who could well afford to bask in the glow of his popularity and take pride in the laughter he had aroused.

PALMER BOVIE

Rutgers University
*April, 1963*

Audio Valerium Martialem deceſſiſſe, & moleſte
fero. Erat homo ingenioſus · acutus, et qui plurimũ in
ſcribendo, & ſalis haberet, & fellis, nec candoris mi
nus. Proſecutus eram uiatico ſecedẽtem · dederam uer
ſiculis, quos de me compoſuit. Fuit moris antiqui, eos,
qui uel ſingulorum laudes, uel uerbũ ſcripſerãt, aut
honoribus, aut pecunia ornare. Noſtris uero tempori
bus, ut alia ſpecioſa, et egregia, ita hoc in primis exole
uit. Nam poſtquam deſiuimus facere laudãda, lauda
ri quoque ineptum putamus. Quæris qui ſint uerſicu
li, quibus gratiam retulerim? mitterẽ ad te ipſum uo
lumen, niſi quoſdã tenerẽ. Tu ſi placuerint hi, cæteros
in libro requires. Alloquitur muſam. Mandat, ut do
mum meam in exquiliis quærat, adeatq; reuerenter.
S ed ne tempore non tuo diſertam
P ulſes ebria ianuam, uideto.
T otos dat tetricæ dies Mineruæ,
D um centum ſtudet auribus uirorum
H oc, quod ſecula, poſteriq; poſſint
A rpinis quoque comparare chartis.
S eras tutior ibis ad lucernas.
H æc hora eſt tua, dum furit Lyæus,
D um regnat roſa, dum madent capilli,
T um me uel rigidi legant Catones.
Meritó ne eũ, qui hoc de me ſcripſit, et tũc dimiſi ami
ciſſime, et nunc amiciſſimum defunctum eſſe doleo? de
dit enim mihi, quãtum maxime potuit daturus ampli
us, ſi potuiſſet. Tæt ſi qd homini põt dari maius, q̃ glo
ria, laus, & æternitas? A eterna, quæ ſcripſit non erũt
fortaſſe. Ille tamen ſcripſit tanquam futura. Vale.

# Pliny the Younger on Martial*

I HAVE JUST HEARD OF THE DEATH of poor Martial, which much concerns me. He was a man of acute genius, and his writings abound in both wit and satire, combined with equal candour. When he left Rome I complimented him by a present to defray the charges of his journey, in return for the little poem which he had written about me. It was the custom of the ancients to distinguish those poets with honours or pecuniary rewards, who had celebrated particular persons or cities in their verses; but this practice, with every other that is fair and noble, is now grown out of fashion; and in consequence of having ceased to act laudably, we consider applause as an impertinent and worthless tribute. You will be desirous, perhaps, to see the verses which merited this acknowledgement from me; and I believe I can, from my memory, partly satisfy your curiosity, without referring you to his works: but

* This letter by Pliny the Younger to Cornelius Priscus was taken from the Aldus Edition of 1504 of *The Works of Pliny*. The facsimile on page 24 shows the original text. This edition was the first in the history of printing to use italic type, an invention of Aldus. The translation was taken from the Loeb Library edition of Pliny's letters (Book III, letter 21), I, 266.

if you are pleased with this specimen of them, you must
turn to his poems for the rest. He addresses himself to his
Muse, whom he directs to seek my house upon the Esquiline,
and to approach me with respect:

> Go, wanton Muse, but go with care,
> Nor meet, ill-tim'd, my Pliny's ear.
> He, by sage Minerva taught,
> Gives the day to studious thought,
> And plans that eloquence divine,
> Which shall to future ages shine,
> And rival, wond'rous Tully! thine.
> Then, cautious, watch the vacant hour,
> When Bacchus reigns in all his power!
> When crown'd with rosy chaplets gay,
> E'en rigid Catos read my lay.

Do you not think that the poet who wrote in such terms of
me, deserved some friendly marks of my bounty then, and
that he merits my sorrow now? For he gave me the most he
could, and it was want of power only, if his present was not
more valuable. But to say truth, what higher can be conferred on man than fame, and applause, and immortality?
And though it should be granted, that his poems will not be
immortal, still, no doubt, he composed them upon the contrary supposition. Farewell.

# Translator's Note

FIFTEEN HUNDRED EPIGRAMS ARE too many, except for the most passionate lover of the definitive collected. So here we have about a tenth that number, a random sampling, about evenly taken from each of the twelve books. Not entirely random, for I have tried to show Martial's variety, while acknowledging that any selection may distort his emphasis. The poems are presented in the order which they chance to follow from the original books; this seems better, if more haphazard, than trying to group by content or style. I chose poems that I liked, or poems that I found tractable, or both. Most of the time, because the tradition of English verse needs rhyme for wit, especially in the shorter poems, I have rhymed, as Martial did not; but I have also brought over some poems in ten-syllable approximations of Martial's hendecasyllabic (eleven syllables) and in elegiac meters. I have had no consistent principle in this matter, nor in my use of anachronisms.

ROLFE HUMPHRIES

# MARTIAL

SELECTED
EPIGRAMS

# From Book I

## I. i

Here he is, the man you read and look for,
Martial, known to fame the whole world over
For his keen little epigrams, twelve volumes.
As I live and breathe, devoted reader,
You give me, alive, such praise and glory
As few poets have when dust and ashes.

## I. x

Gemellus wants to marry Maronilla,
Cajoles, implores, and even sends her presents.
—Is she so lovely? —No, an utter horror.
—What's the attraction, then? —Her cough is awful.

## I. xvi

Some so-so things, some bad, some good ones here,
And that's the way a book is made, old dear.

### I. xxiv

You see that fellow with the shaggy hair,
Ranting about old heroes and their might,
Whose gloomy frown gives all the girls a scare?
Don't trust his looks—he wás a bride last night.


### I. xxvii

Last night (I had downed a fifth, or nearly)
I said, "Why not dine with me tomorrow?"
You at once assumed the thing was settled,
Noting—what a dangerous example!—
My intoxicated invitation.
What I hate about a fellow tippler
Is a perfect memory, Procillus.


### I. xxviii

If anybody thinks
Acerra always stinks
Of yesterday's sour wine,
The man is out of line.
Acerra always drinks
Until the morning blinks.

I. xxx

Diaulus was once a physician,
But later became a mortician.
Bed rest, as before,
He prescribes, only more—
An exceedingly minor transition.


I. xxxii

I do not like you, Sabidius.
It's not that I'm overfastidious,
And if you ask why,
I can only reply,
*I do not like you, Sabidius.*

## I. lv

Fronto, bright ornament of peace and war,
If you would know what Martial's wishes are,
He'd like to till his own estate and be
Proprietor of rough security.
What idiot would delight in chilly halls,
With "Greetings!," as some morning client calls,
When fields and woods might furnish his desire,
Or he unpacks his creel before the fire?
With quivering rod he takes the leaping trout,
A reddish crock pours golden honey out,
The table wobbles, but it's loaded down
By a fat cook, with foods not bought in town.
Let those who hate me and this kind of life
Dwell, pale-faced wretches, in the city strife.


## I. lvii

What kind of a girl, you ask, do I find most easy to follow?
    One not too easy to make, one not too terribly coy.
Something halfway between the two extremes I approve of—
    Neither a tart nor a tease, Flaccus, is what I enjoy.

I. lxiv

You're beautiful, oh yes, and young, and rich;
But since you tell us so, you're just a bitch.


I. lxxxvi

Novius lives next door, and I can almost
Reach my hand and touch him from my window.
Who'd not envy me, not think me lucky
All the time, with such a boon companion
Living so close by for my enjoyment?
Yet he seems as far from me as Terence
On the river Nile, lord of Syene.
I can't dine with him, I never see him,
Never even hear him. In the city
No one seems as near and far as he does.
One of us will have to do some moving.
If you never want a glimpse of Novius,
You should be his neighbor, or his roommate.

I. cvii

Often, my dearly beloved Lucius Julius, you nag me:
  "Write something grand for a change; oh, what a loafer
    you are!"
Give me a life of ease, the kind that Vergil and Horace
  Once on a time enjoyed, the gift of Maecenas their lord.
Then I would try to provide works that would live through
    the ages,
  Works that would render my name safe from the funeral
    flame.
Oxen won't carry the yoke into fields that are salted and
    barren—
  In a luxurious soil, how delightful the toil!

# From Book II

## II. v

Yes, Decianus, I'd delight
To be with you by day, by night.
The miles between us, me and you,
As we both know, are only two.
But if I call in vain, two more
Are added on, and that makes four.
Often you're not at home, and when
You are, they tell me, "Call again!",
"He's resting," "He's in conference"—
Am I that dumb? Am I that dense?
I'd gladly walk a mile or two
If I could count on seeing you,
But when I have to hoof it four
*Not* to have seen you—what a bore!

## II. ix

I wrote. No answer. Nothing doing. Still,
Naevia read my letter. So—she will.

## II. xi

Behold, how Selius wears a clouded brow
And paces up and down the colonnade.
His looks betray his melancholy now,
His ugly chin upon his chest is laid,
His right hand beats his breast or tears his hair,
And yet he mourns no friend or brother lost,
His sons both live—*long may they* is my prayer—
No tenant's failed, no agent double-crossed
His household, sound as any one's in Rome.
What is the trouble, then?—He dines at home.

## II. xx

Paulus pays cash for poems. No other right
Than purchase gives him warrant to recite.

## II. xxi

Kisses to some, to others your hand to shake,
You offer, Postumus. I know which I'll take.

II. xxxi

I've often had Christine. "What kind of lay
Is she?," you ask. Out of this world, I'd say.


II. xxxv

Your legs curve like a crescent moon,
    And sure as you are born,
Phoebus, you could wash your feet
    In any drinking horn.


II. xxxviii

What good's a farm so far from anywhere?
One thing, at least. I don't see Linus there.


II. xli

"Laugh, girl, laugh, if you are wise."
Ovid (I guess) gave this advice,
But Ovid did not say this to
All of the girls, including you;
For girlishness is what you lack,
Maxine, and your three teeth are black.

So, trust your looking glass and me,
And be as much afraid of glee
As Spanius dreads a breeze that may
Blow off his elegant toupée,
As Priscus shudders, lest a touch
Disorganize his clothes too much,
As rain would terrify Sabella,
Chalk-powdered, under her umbrella,
Or as Fabulla fears the sun
With her white-leaded lacquer on.
Put on the look that gives men pause,
Like Hecuba's, or Katisha's,
Avoid Philistion's funny cracks,
And parties where behavior's lax.
Don't let inelegant guffaws
Unhinge the portals of your jaws.
The place for you, believe me, kiddo,
Is with an orphan or a widow,
A bride bereft, a grieving groom,
Or any paragon of gloom.
What more than this can I advise?—
*Weep, girl, weep, if you are wise.*

## II. xlviii

A barman and a butcher and a bath,
A barber, a backgammon board (with dice),
Books, not too many, but of my selection,
One boon companion, not too crude a person,
A nice tall boy, not prematurely bearded,
A broad, or babe, the boy can find delight in,
Bestow these on me, even at Butunti,
And, Rufus, you can keep the baths of Nero.

## II. lii

Spatale's a full-breasted lady,
    So buxom and so bosomy
That when she buys a bathing ticket,
    The cashier makes her pay for three.

## II. lxxx

Fannius, fleeing from a foe,
    Committed suicide.
What folly! To escape from death,
    Fannius up and died.

## II. lxxxvii

Sextus, you claim that pretty girls all burn
With passionate love of you, and seethe, and simmer
Infatuated by a boob whose face
Reminds me of an underwater swimmer.

# From Book III

## III. viii

"Quintus loves Thais." "Which Thais?" "Thais, the girl
    with one eye."
  Thais is lacking one eye; Quintus is totally blind.

## III. ix

Cinna writes verse against me. So I've heard.
But—do you write, if no one reads a word?

## III. x

Your father, Philomusus, used to pay,
As your allowance, half a fin a day
And every day shelled out that sum or more
Since you were broke at sundown, or before.
Dying, he left you every cent he had.
Oh, oh! You're disinherited, my lad.

### III. xiv

Starving, Don Tuccius left for Rome,
    Turning his back on Spain,
And heard about the clients' dole,
    And came right home again.

### III. xviii

You say, to start with, you have laryngitis;
Stop right there, Maximus, and you'll delight us.

### III. xxv

Sabinus, our distinguished rhetorician,
Has such a subantarctic disposition
That when he jumps in the hot baths of Nero,
The temperature goes promptly down to zero.

### III. xxxv

Phidias carved the fish around the rim
Of this fine bowl. Add water, and they'll swim.

### III. xli

On the bowl's rim, by Mentor's art portrayed,
The lizard seems alive; my hand's afraid.

### III. xliv

Nobody ever, it seems, is glad to meet you,
And at your arrival, Ligurinus,
Flight and monstrous solitude surround you.
Why?, you wonder. You're too much the poet.
This is indeed the deadliest of failings.
Not a tigress when her cubs are stolen,
Not a viper, swollen hot in sunshine,
Not a scorpion is half as dreaded.
Who, I ask you, could endure such trials?
You insist on reading to me, always,
Reading when I'm standing, when I'm sitting,
When I'm on the run, or in the backhouse.
In the Turkish bath, you make my ears ring,
In the pool, I have no chance of swimming,
On my way to eat, you grab and stop me,
At my meal you drive me from the table,
If I'm tired and sleepy, you arouse me.
Won't you see the trouble you are causing?
Here you are, a good man, honest, upright,
Decent, just, and yet—a holy terror!

### III. xlix

Massic for you, Veian for me. I think
I'd rather smell your cup than taste my drink.

### III. liii

Your face, neck, hands, legs, bosom, buttocks, thighs,
Are nothing, Chloe, that we greatly prize.
Details are needless; by this time you know we
Could do without the total of you, Chloe.

### III. lxiv

The Sirens brought to mariners
A happy doom, a joyful knell,
A lovely death, and none who heard
Ever escaped their singing spell
Except Ulysses; let me say
This strikes me with much less surprise
Than if I heard he'd got away
From Canius' longwinded lies.

III. lvi

Ravenna's climate is so beastly dry
That wine is cheap, but water very high.

III. xc

Galla wants to, doesn't want to,
    Eeny, meeny, miny, mo.
Does she, don't she, will she, won't she—
    How the hell am I to know?

# From Book IV

IV. ii

Alone of all the people there,
Horace wore black to watch the show.
Commoners, knights, and emperor
Shone in their white, row after row.
From every quarter of the sky
A sudden, swirling snowstorm pressed,
And Horace, watching, found his cloak
Was just as white as all the rest.


IV. viii

In the first hour, and second, clients tire
Making their morning duty calls; the third
Sends the hoarse-voiced attorneys to the courts.
Till the fifth hour Rome tends her various tasks,
Then rests from sixth to seventh; oily wrestlers
Practice their holds and counters for an hour.
By then it's time to let our bodies rest
On soft-piled couches, and the tenth hour seems
The time to read my little book of poems.

Euphemus, when your courtesy has set
The ambrosial feast, and kindly Caesar soothes
His mood with heaven's nectar, his great hand
Around the half-full cup, that's time for jokes.
—My Muse has some reluctance about coming
To meet a solemn Jove at early morning.

## IV. xii

To no one you say, *No!* Thais, that's fine,
But are there acts at which you draw the line?

## IV. xxi

"There are no gods, Heaven is empty space,"
So Segius claims, and amply proves his case,
For certainly no decent deity
Would grant him all his new prosperity.

IV. xxiv

Lycoris seems to have a longer life
Than all her friends. I wish she liked my wife.


IV. xxxviii

Refuse me, Galla—teasing keeps love strong,
But don't refuse me, Galla, for too long.


IV. xliv

Here is Vesuvius, green, not long ago, with its shadows;
    Here from patrician grapes came the aristocrat wine;
Here were the ridges that Bacchus loved more than the
        foothills of Nysa;
    Here on the mountainside Satyrs would leap in the dance;
Here was Venus' abode, a realm more dear than her Sparta.
    Here was the site of a town famous for Hercules' name.
Now it all lies choked and quenched under desolate ashes,
    Even the gods on high wish no such license were theirs.

IV. xlvi

Christmas has made Sabellus rich.
He proudly claims he would not switch
With any Roman counsellor,
But what's he so conceited for?
These are his gifts: a quart or two
Of beans mashed up with spelt; a few
Peppers, a little frankincense;
Sausages worth, say, fifty cents;
A haggis, and a hunk of tripe,
Some dates from Lybia (overripe),
A Syrian flagon, full of lees,
Some onions, snails, and cottage cheese.
From a Picenian client came
A little box whose splintered frame
Might hold five olives and a fig
If none of them were very big.
Then, from Saguntum, far away,
Came seven crude mugs of Spanish clay
And a napkin, with such stripèd hues
As only senators may use.
A prouder Christmas, it appears,
Has not been his these past ten years.

IV. lxiv

More blessed than the gardens where
The golden apples used to grow
Are these few acres, looking down
From their high ridge to hills below.
This area, with its graceful swell,
Enjoys a more untroubled height,
And when the valleys fill with cloud
Shines with its own peculiar light.
How near the undiluted stars
Beam on the graces of this home,
Whence we may see the Seven Hills,
May estimate the scope of Rome.
Beyond lie Alba, Tusculum,
And all the cool, suburban shade,
Anna Perenna's fruitful grove
Where virgins wanton, unafraid,
Fidenae, Rubrae, and the roads
To salty marsh or higher ground
With traffic moving north or south.
From here, the wagons make no sound,
No axle-creak is borne this high,
And though the Mulvian Bridge is near,
Where sailors bawl and bargemen shout,
You sleep in peace. You do not hear.
You watch, far off, the vessels glide

In their slow motion down the stream,
The holy Tiber.
                              Country place?
Familiar mansion of your dream?
Whichever it is, its owner-host
Conveys to you, in simple fee,
Unenvious, his warmth of heart,
His genial hospitality.
Ulysses' host, or Hercules',
Was no more lavish. All of you
Who deem all this of small account,
Go on to Tivoli, and subdue
Her coolness with your hundred hoes;
Make Setia one man's holding; praise
High Palestrina's citadels,
But let my taste prefer these fields
Where Julius Martialis dwells.


## IV. lxix

You serve the most expensive wine,
And rumor says it's very fine,
And some three times, or was it four,
Its virtues made you bachelor.
Papylus, this is false, I think,
I almost know: still—I'll not drink.

IV. lxxxiv

Thais, whom no tailchaser ever lays,
Is evil-tongued. But not in what she says.

IV. lxxxvii

Bassa constantly plumps a cute little kiddie beside her,
    Calls it her plaything, her dear, calls it the joy of her heart.
Bassa (perhaps you're surprised) is far from devoted to
        toddlers:
Why does she put on this act? Bassa's too ready to fart.

# From Book V

## V. ix

I wasn't well; so, Dr. S., you led
A hundred of your interns to my bed.
Two hundred chilly paws assailed my brow;
I had no fever, but I have one now.

## V. xviii

In drear-nighted December
The napkins fly around,
And slender spoons, and tapers,
And paper by the pound,
And jars of dried-up damsons
To please the taste of cooks,
While I have sent you nothing
But homespun little books.
Don't think me rude or stingy,
I hate the craft, the guile,
The trickery of presents
Which have a fishhook style.

You know how trout are taken
When rising to the lure:
To give your rich friend nothing
Is generous, if you're poor.


## V. xx

If you and I, dear Martial,
Enjoying carefree days,
Were free to join our leisure
And walk in gracious ways,
We should avoid the mansions
Where men of power dwell,
The lawsuits of the forum
And all that bustling hell.
The malls, the parks, the lounges,
The gardens, an arcade
Where one might find a bookshop
Would be our promenade.
Cold baths from Aqua Virgo
Or warmer ones in town,
These are the places, always,
To lay our burdens down.
Neither of us is living
The way things are today;
We see the good suns going,
The brightness fall away.

We waste our time's allowance,
And Time does not forgive.
Why waste one precious moment
If we know how to live?


### V. xxiv

Hermes, in whom all sons of Mars delight,
Hermes, adept in every kind of fight,
Hermes, both teacher and a fighting fool,
Hermes, the terrorist of his own school,
Hermes, the only one who Helius cows,
Hermes, to whom alone Advolans bows,
Hermes, who wins, yet does not kill his foe,
Hermes, who needs no substitute, we know,
Hermes, the ticket-speculators' joy,
Hermes, the female fans' drooled-over boy,
Hermes, the master of the warlike spear,
Hermes, who glowers with terrifying sneer,
Hermes, on horseback terrible and grim,
Hermes, what gladiator equals him?
Hermes, the glory of the world of Mars,
Hermes, the avatar of avatars,
Hermes, supreme with trident and the net,
Hermes, our Three in one, our Triple Threat—
Yea, Hermes!

V. xxxiv

Fronto my father, to you and my mother Flacilla I tender
  This little servingmaid, joy and delight of my heart.
Don't let her shiver and shake in the shadowy blackness of
    Hades,
  Don't let her be afraid of the Hell-hound's horrible jaws.
She had arrived, almost, at one more of her few winter
    birthdays,
  She would have lived six years, given another six days.
Now let her romp as she will in the sight of her agèd
    protectors,
  Let her lisping voice utter the sound of my name.
Let the turf above her delicate bones lie gently;
  Rest on her lightly, O Earth, on whom her step was so
    light.


V. xxxvi

A man I praised, Faustinus, in a book
Claims that he owes me nothing. What a crook!

V. xlvii

Philo has never dined at home,
  He'll swear, and he'll repeat.
True. When he cannot cadge a meal,
  Philo just doesn't eat.

V. lii

Your kindnesses I prize, and always will,
But since you talk about them, I keep still.
No sooner, Postumus, do I start to praise
Some gift of yours, when my companion says,
"I know—he told me." What am I to do?
Some things do not require the praise of two.
Keep still, or let me talk. All gifts are less
When givers comment on them to excess.

## V. lvi

To whom should you entrust your son
For further ed-u-ca-ti-on?
Well, first of all, Lupus, I'd say,
Keep him implacably away
From pedagogues whose lectures stick
To *Elements of Rhetoric*;
Let him abjure, forswear, ignore
Vergil, and that profounder bore
Named Marcus Tullius Cicero;
If he writes verse, the little schmo
Should be cut off without a cent,
But if he's properly intent
On piling up a mound of loot,
Get him to play the harp or flute.
If he is dull of intellect,
He'd better be an architect
Or find a lucrative career
As a loud-bawling auctioneer.

V. lviii

Tomorrow you say you will live; *tomorrow* you always are
    saying.
  Postumus, tell me the truth; when does "Tomorrow"
    arrive?
How far away is it now? where are we going to find it?
  Surely it doesn't lie hid in the midst of Armenian hosts!
That Tomorrow of yours is as ancient as Nestor or Priam;
  What would a man have to pay to have that Tomorrow
    today?
Tomorrow you're going to live? But living today's none too
    early,
  And the really wise man has had yesterday's living for
    sure.


V. lxviii

This lock of hair, from far beyond the Rhone,
Proves, dear, how much more golden is your own.

### V. lxxiii

Why don't I send my books to you
When you've asked me so many times?
Good enough reason, Ted; you might
Reciprocate with your own rhymes.

### V. lxxxi

If you are poor, you'll always be that way;
Only the rich get richer in our day.

# From Book VI

Fabulla swears the hair she buys is hers:
Does that place her among the perjurers?

Mine's no case of murder, mayhem, poison,
But three she-goats, and I claim my neighbor stole them.
That's all right, says the judge, but you have to prove it.
You sound off about Hannibal and Carthage.
Days that will live in infamy forever,
Our heroic Mariuses and Sullas,
With a big loud voice and the most expansive
Far-flung sweep of the ultimate in gesture.
Aw, now, Counsellor—talk about the three goats.

### VI. xxiii

You tell me, Lesbia, always be prepared
To rise to all occasions whatsoever,
You urge me on by hand, by coaxing words,
But your face adjures me, *Never!*

### VI. xxxi

You know your doctor likes to give your wife
Treatments that everybody knows relieve her.
Charidemus, you must want to end your life
By poison, not by fever.

### VI. xxxiii

What's happened to Sabellus,
Who used to be so "gay"?
His slaves get dead, or rob him,
They also run away,
And fires and floods depress him,
He feels so out of luck
That in his desperation,
Poor wretch, he'll even practice normal intercourse.

VI. xxxv

You ask for seven water clocks
As time in which to plead.
The judge is none too pleased with this,
But sourly says, "Agreed!"
So you go on, and on, and on,
And, heated by your task,
You pause for one long, lukewarm swig
Of water from your flask.
Cecil, for God's sake, kill two birds
With just one stone, or rock,
And end your thirst and speech alike—
Drink from the water clock!


VI. xli

He who endeavors to recite
With throat and neck both bandaged tight
Proves, with a most insistent will,
That he can't speak, and won't keep still.


VI. xliv

You think you have a most amusing wit
And overflow with flooding streams of it,

You sneer at all of us, Calliodorus,
Confident that your rudenesses don't bore us.
Let me point out one thing—you know it's true—
No one hands on the cup in pledge to you.


### VI. xlvi

Ben Hur is plying the whip with all his might,
Yet the Blue chariot never seems to hurry.
Since his left hand is stronger than his right,
Betters on other colors need not worry.


### VI. liii

With us he bathed and dined, highspirited,
Yet by next morn Andragoras was dead.
The cause?—According to the autopsies,
He dreamed he saw Doctor Hermocrates.


### VI. lxvi

A girl of none too nice renown,
The kind you often see down town,
An auctioneer had up for sale,
But bidding languished, seemed to fail,

And so, to prove her pure and sweet,
And almost good enough to eat,
While she pretended to resist,
He drew her closer to him, kissed
Her on the mouth, three times, then four,
To prove his point so much the more.
You ask what good this kissing did?
—The highest man withdrew his bid.

### VI. lxx

Cotta is over sixty years
Or maybe sixty-two
And can't recall a single day
When he was down with flu.
At Alcon and at Dasius,
Our leading medicoes,
He thrusts the insulting finger out,
And also thumbs his nose.
While as for us, subtract our days
Of kidney stones and cough,
The hours prostration nullified
Or fevers carried off,
What have we left? A dozen years
From aches and ailments free,
And we appear old men. You're wrong
To think longevity

Requires a Nestor's length of days,
A Priam's passing bell—
Life does not lie in living long
So much as living well.


### VI. lxxxii

A certain fellow looked me over,
Like a slave buyer, or a scout
For gladiators, eyed me closely,
Put down a note, and then called out,
"Are you," he said, "are you that Martial
Whom everybody with an ear
Knows for his jokes and double meanings?"
I gave a modest smirk, or leer,
And with a little bow, admitted
That I was that celebrity.
"Then why do you wear a cloak as awful
As that one you have on?" said he.
I answered, "I'm an awful poet,"
But lest this kind of thing go on
Too often, kindly send me, Rufus,
A better cloak that I can don.

# From Book VII

## VII. iv

His pale complexion changed from bad to worse,
So Oppian began composing verse.

## VII. ix

Cascellius is sixty years of age.
He's clever. Will he ever be a sage?

## VII. xix

This fragment, which you scorn as useless wood,
Was the first keel across an unknown sea,
Part of the good ship *Argo*, which withstood
The Clashing Rocks, the Pontic's savagery,
Worn down to this by time, more precious now
Than, once, from keel to mast, from stern to prow.

### VII. xxxi

Fowls from the cackling yard, and eggs,
Yellow unripened Chian figs,
The offspring of a bleating dam
(I mean a kid and not a lamb),
Frost bitten olives, cabbages—
How wrong you are to think that these
Are sent you from the farm I own.
I am the only thing there grown.
Whatever your Umbrian tenant sends,
Or that estate whose border ends
Three miles from town, whatever yield
Is yours from your Etruscan field—
Can I produce such harvests? No, sir,
I get them from the nearest grocer.

### VII. xxxvi

When my country shack no longer resisted the rainstorms
   When it started to swim under the wintry floods,
You sent a load of tiles to repel and discourage the
    cloudbursts,
   Yours was the generous hand keeping the roof overhead.

Now December roars harsh with Boreas' thunder,
    Stella, the house, it seems is better protected than I.
Couldn't you let me have a raincoat or secondhand poncho,
    Almost any old rag, Stella, for keeping me dry?

VII. xxxix

Caelius could endure no longer
The frantic rushing all about
To call on supercilious patrons,
And so he claimed he had the gout,
Taped up his feet, and limped and hobbled,
And bought prescriptions by the score,
So pretty soon—powers of suggestion!—
He wasn't faking any more.

### VII. xlvi

While you are striving to write a poem to go with your
     present,
   While you strive to compose better than Homer himself,
Priscus, day after day you are hurting yourself, and you hurt
     me;
   If your muse remains dumb, when is my present to come?
Send to the men who are rich the elegant strains of
     Parnassus;
   Prose is all right to send with a gift for an indigent friend.

### VII. xlix

These little gifts from my suburban site:
Eggs for your need, apples for your delight.

VII. lxi

Shopkeepers—what a nerve!—had robbed us of all of the
    city,
  Never a threshold stayed on its own side of the sill.
Your edict has changed all that, Your Majesty; streets have
    been widened,
  Narrow trails are replaced by roads we can travel at will.
Pillar and post no more are decorated with flagons,
  Praetors don't have to walk out in the muck and the mud,
Razors aren't wielded and plied around barberchairs set on
    the sidewalk,
  Nor do the butchershop hands spatter the pavement with
    blood.
Rome is a city again, no longer a pushcart market,
  Barber and barman and cook stay where they bloody well
    should.


VII. lxxvii

"Give me your poems!," you demand,
Tucca, but I'll not heed.
You want to sell them secondhand,
You don't intend to read.

### VII. lxxxiii

Bill Quick's a barber, but he has the slows:
While he shaves off one beard, another grows.

### VII. xc

Matho complains that my book is more than a little uneven;
  If he is telling the truth, then he is praising my pen.
Books that are even throughout, Matho, are sure to be
    dreadful;
  Books without height and depth come from the stupidest
    men.

### VII. xciv

Once there was perfume in this little jar;
Paphylus sniffed; it turned to vinegar.

## VII. xcv

It's winter, and hoary December
Roughens with frost and with snow,
Yet you, with your icy kisses,
Linus, wherever you go,
Slobber on all of the Romans.
What more sadistic return
Could you make in exchange for a beating?
Even my wife I would spurn
Or my little innocent daughter,
With her flattering lips, in this cold,
But you are more subtly attractive,
Of course, and your dog nostrils hold
An icicle, pendent and livid,
And your beard is as stiff in its coat
Of ice as the kind that a barber
Cuts off an African goat.
I can honestly say that I'd rather
Meet up with a hundred or more
Of—never mind what; I'm less frightened
By Cybele's priesthood; therefore,
Linus, I beg and entreat you,
If you have any shame or goodwill,
Put off those refrigerant kisses
Till April has melted the chill.

# From Book VIII

### VIII. x

A Tyrian cloak of the most precious dye
Was sold to Bassus just the other day,
Priced at five hundred dollars. What a buy!
"A bargain?" "Sure—Bassus will never pay."

### VIII. xvi

A baker, once, Cyperus, now
You are a counsellor, and how!
That you are prosperous is clear
From your ten thousand bucks a year,
But—here today and gone tomorrow!—
You're constantly compelled to borrow.
Your old profession, as we know,
You don't forsake, still needing dough.

## VIII. xx

Two hundred lines a day
Varus is said to write.
We're grateful for the way
He never will recite.
This proves he's halfway bright.

## VIII. xxii

You bid me to a beefsteak meal,
But all you serve is scraggly veal.
I'm a dumb ox, but even so,
Gallicus, don't you think I know?

## VIII. xxv

You came to see me only once
When I was sick in bed.
I thank you, Oppian; had you come
More often, I'd be dead.

### VIII. xxvii

He who gives presents to a rich old man,
Like you, for instance, Gaurus—never doubt it—
Is telling you as plainly as he can,
"Kindly drop dead, and hurry up about it!"

### VIII. xxxv

Alike in your disgusting lives
Oh, worst of husbands, worst of wives,
I'm more than puzzled when I see
Your incompatibility.

### VIII. xliii

Fabius buries his wives, Chrestilla buries her husbands,
    Each of them waving the torch over a newly-wed's couch.
Venus, bring them together; a tie is the meed for such
        winners,
    Happy as husband and bride, one in the funeral ride.

### VIII. liii

Loveliest of all women past and present,
And lewdest of all women past and present,
Oh, how I wish, Catulla, you would be
Less lovely, or more bent on decency.

### VIII. lxviii

The orchards of Corcyra's king
Are less spectacular than those,
Entellus, which your walls enclose.
Here, lest the hateful northers bring
Cold winter-burning to the vine,
Or lest the chilly frost consume
The gift of Bacchus, future wine,
Your vineyards, with protected bloom,
Behind transparent window walls,
Flourish protected, fair to see,
And fortunate, whate'er befalls.
So, through her silken drapery,
One sees the radiance and gleam
Of a girl's limbs; so one may look
Below the slowly moving brook
And count the pebbles in the stream.
Nature from one ingenious wit
Withholds invention; here we find

The barren winter benefit
Autumn, obedient to man's mind.


## VIII. lxix

You praise dead poets only. Very nice!
Vacerra, I don't want to pay that price.


## VIII. lxxiv

Oculist once, and now a gladiator—
No change, except the new arena's greater.


## VIII. lxxix

Fabulla, all your female friends
Are hags or uglier than hags.
To parties, colonnades, and shows
You drag these horrible old bags,
And people say, where'er you go,
"Isn't Fabulla lovely, though?"

# From Book IX

## IX. v

Paula, it comes to me as no surprise
You want to marry Priscus; you are wise.
But Priscus doesn't want to marry you,
Which goes to prove, I'd say, that he's wise, too.

## IX. x

Although you like to dine away from home,
You bawl abuse like any oxen-goader.
Cantharus, cut it out, pipe down. In Rome
Free speech is not accorded a freeloader.

## IX. xv

"Chloe wrought this," we see engraved in stone
Over the tombs of seven husbands gone:
Was accusation ever more clearly shown?

IX. xviii

I have, and by your grace I hope to keep,
Caesar, my dwellings in and out of town,
But the curved pole, bucket, and swinging sweep
Hardly suffice to wet my garden down.
My house complains that it is worse than dry
Though the great Marcian flume is rushing near:
Grant water to my household gods, and I
Will think Jove's golden rain descended here.


IX. xix

In some three hundred lines of verse you praise
The baths of Ponticus. (His feasts are good.)
Don't think, Sabellus, I mistake your ways:
It's not a bath you really want, but food.


IX. xxxiii

If you're passing the baths and you hear,
From within, an uproarious cheer,
You may safely conclude
Maron's there, in the nude,
With that tool which has nowhere a peer.

IX. xxxv

By such arts as these, Philomusus, you work for your
    dinners,
  Making up lie after lie, passing them on as the truth.
You know what Pacorus the king plots in his Parthian
    palace,
  You can count to a man the armies from east of the
    Rhine.
You can break, in your mind, the code of the Dacian
    commander;
  Winners and losers you know, ages before the event.
Weatherwise, too—you can tell how often it rains in Syene,
  How many ships set sail loaded with Libyan grain.
You can predict which brows will be graced with the
    Emperor's olive,
  You can divine for whom Jupiter fashions his crown.
Ah, cut it out, Philomusus; come, join me today for a
    dinner—
  There's one catch to it, though; you mustn't tell what
    you know.

IX. xlv

A soldier, Marcellinus, you campaign
Under the rigors of the Northern Wain
And the slow-wheeling stars of Getic skies.
Behold, how near the compass of your eyes
Towers, now, Prometheus' crag of tumbled stones!
You'll see the rocks that echoed with his groans,
And, as you look at them, no doubt you will
Remind yourself," But he was harder still!"
And you may add, "His all-enduring powers
Gave him the right to mould this race of ours."


IX. xlvi

Gellius has an edifice complex.
He's always building, cellars or sundecks,
Purchasing bolts and bars, and fitting keys,
Altering window frames, now those, now these,
Building forever, building without end,
His "Building!" fixes every borrowing friend.

### IX. lii

Believe me, Quintus, I commend
Your April Kalends, even more
Than mine in March, the month before.
We mark with stones of shining white
Our birthdays, source of life and light.
March gave me life, April a friend—
Your Kalends, Quintus, gave me more.

### IX. lxii

Philaenis, night and day,
Wears garments drenched in dye,
Not that she's so soignée,
But Tyrian dyes, they say,
Outrank Philaenis' smell:
This serves Philaenis well.

### IX. lxviii

Why can't you let us be, you damned schoolmaster,
Obnoxious to the girls and to the boys?
The roosters have no more than started crowing
When you begin your beatings and your noise.
Brass bangs no louder on the smitten anvils
Which some equestrian statue-maker pounds,
And there's less uproar in the Coliseum
When the shields clash and wild applause resounds.
Sleep all night long your neighbors do not ask for,
But daylight rousing isn't right at all;
Send home your pupils, wide mouth; let us pay you
As much for silence as you get to bawl.

### IX. lxxxi

Readers and listeners enjoy my books,
But poet Whozis thinks I'm pretty crude.
I don't much care. I'd rather have my food
Appeal to hungry feasters than to cooks.

# From Book X

X. viii

Paula wants to marry me;
*I won't*, I've often told her.
She's an old woman, but I might,
If she were only older.

X. xi

Calliodorus, you gabble of nothing but lofty-souled heroes,
  Thinking yourself the peer of Pylades and other great
    men.
I'll be damned if you're fit to pass Pylades a pisspot,
  Nor to sling swill to the pigs Pirithous had in his pen.
"Ah, but," I hear you say, "I once gave a friend twenty
    dollars,
  Also a shirt I had worn two or three times, maybe four."
What do you think real friends have to do with handing out
    presents?
  Giving, no matter how much, for you means withholding
    much more.

### X. xxiii

Happy in peaceful old age, Antonius Primus can reckon
  Fifteen Olympiads gone, five and seventy years.
Looking back on the past, on his panorama of decades,
  Calm and serene he smiles, while the current of Lethe
    nears.
Not one day of the past, he reflects, was hateful or gloomy,
  Never a bygone time he is not glad to recall.
So, a good man's years are prolonged, and he has them twice
    over
  When he can summon them back, doubly enjoying them
    all.

### X. xl

My Polla, people often said,
Was cheating on me with a sodomite.
I caught the pair of them in bed—
The story simply wasn't right!

### X. xlvii

Here are the things, dear friend, which make
Life not impossible to take:
Riches bequeathed, not won by toil;
Fire on the hearth; responsive soil;
No law suits; seldom formal dress;
A frank but wise disarmingness;
A healthy body, and a mind
Alert, but peaceably inclined;
Congenial guests; a table set
Without excessive etiquette;
Nights free from exigence and worry,
But not too bleary or too blurry;
In bed, a wife not frigid nor
Too reminiscent of a whore;
Slumber, to make the shadows swift;
Contentment with your native gift;
And, without longing or dismay,
The prospect of your final day.

### X. liii

Scorpus am I, the glory of your games,
Noisily hailed by your short-lasting cheers.
At twenty-seven, dead. Those foolish dames,
The Fates, mistook my victories for my years.

### X. lxii

Schoolmaster, give your simple mob a break
So that the curly-headed crowds may take
Delight in what you say, and come to you
In throngs no shorthand teacher ever drew.
Under the Lion's sign the white-hot sky
Burns to a crisp the harvests of July.
Put down the rawhide whip, the rubber hose,
The ferule, and the knuckle-duster—those
Should have a rest and sleep until next fall.
Erase the problems on the blackboard wall.
If boys keep well in summer, it's agreed,
They're learning all the lessons that they need.

### X. lxxxvi

No mistress ever burned a man with all
The ardor Laurus felt for playing ball,
And in his day he was a star, no doubt.
What is he now? The All-Etruscan out.

### X. xci

Almo has eunuchs all around the house,
And he himself can't rise to the occasion,

Yet he complains that his beloved spouse
Does nothing to increase the population.


### X. xciv


No dragon watches my Hesperides.
I am no King Alcinous. Instead,
My orchard, gnarled Nomentan apple trees,
Need fear no thief, the fruits are wrinkled lead.
I send you, therefore, from my autumn store
Russets, new-purchased at a downtown store.


### X. xcv


Your husband, Galla, sent you back the brat.
So did your lover. That, I guess, is that.


### X. xcvii


While the pyre was prepared, with sticks and papyrus for
        kindling,
    While his weeping wife was buying up cassia and myrrh,
When the grave, and the bier, and the undertaker were ready,
    Numa made me his heir, signed the will—and got well.

### X. ciii

Does the praise of the name of your poet please and delight
    you,
  Fellow townsmen of mine, sons of the mountain town,
Bilbilis, far above the rushing waters of Salo?
  I am your glory and pride, I am your fame and renown.
Verona owes no more to the delicate gift of Catullus,
  Were I her poet and son, Verona would welcome me home.
Now it is thirty years, more or less, that I have been absent,
  Far from your simple ways, walled by the grandeur of
    Rome.
That is a wonderful town, and I have been happy to be there,
  Under Italian skies, growing older and gray.
If you'll welcome me home, with graciousness, I shall be
    coming;
  If you are churlish of heart, I would do better to stay.

# From Book XI

## XI. xiii

O traveller, faring north from Rome,
Do not pass by this noble tomb.
The city's joy, the wit of Nile,
Pleasure, delight, and art, and style,
The pride and glory of our age,
The sorrow of the Roman stage,
And all the charms the Loves devise
Lie in this tomb where Paris lies.

## XI. xviii

You have given me, Lupus, a suburban tract,
A farm near town. The only thing it lacked
Was acreage. One flower pot, or two,
Contains more land: a single leaf of rue
Is here Diana's grove; a cricket's wing,
Spread out, would shadow almost everything;
An ant could eat our produce in a day,
And one rose petal keep the sun away

Grass is no more abundant on the scene,
Than herbs for spice, or peppers, red and green.
No cucumber can stretch its full length out;
If there's one snake, he doubles up, no doubt;
A caterpillar, here, would not get fat,
Nor this poor fare suffice to glut a gnat.
A mole's my ditcher and my ploughman both,
Where figs and mushrooms can't plump out in growth.
A fieldmouse raids my borders, and is more
Alarming than the Calydonian boar,
The swallow, in his talons, flies away
With all the crop, a frightful bird of prey.
Lopped of his sickle and his yard of broom,
Priapus, still, can find no standing room.
The harvest, gathered in, would never swell
Nor bulge the sides of the minutest shell.
As for the wine, we have a vintage which
We seal inside a walnut smeared with pitch.
Next time it might be better, you'll agree,
Lupus, if you'd omit the *simple fee*,
Or to the last word add a final D.

XI. xxxii

You have no toga, and you have no fire,
No slave, old man or boy, for your desire,
No bug-infested bed, no reedy mat,
No key, no bolt, no mug, no dog, no cat,
Yet, Nestor, you have aspirations; you
Want to appear as one whom people praise
For poverty, and so be kept in view,
"A poor but honest man," for all your days.
What an old fraud and self-deluding fake
You are! It's beggardom, for Heaven's sake,
Not poverty, to have no stick nor stone,
Splinter nor pebble, you can call your own.


XI. xxxv

Three hundred guests, whom I don't know, invited
To dinner at your house, and you feel slighted,
Fabullus, and complain if I decline.
—I don't like being lonesome when I dine.

## XI. lv

Lupus implores you to become a sire.
Urbicus, that's a fraudulent desire.
Legacy hunters always wish for you
The opposite of what they say they do.
If your Cosconia should announce some day,
"I'm pregnant," he would almost pass away.
Take his advice, or seem to, and pass on
So that he'll think you must have left a son.

## XI. lxii

Lesbia swears she never was laid for free.
Correct—she always had to pay the fee.

## XI. lxiv

Faustus, I don't know what you write
    To all the girls in town;
I do know what they don't write you—
    "Dear Faustus:

                    Please come down!"

XI. lxvi

You inform and you blackmail,
You're a pimp and a cheat;
Off a stable of wrestlers
You manage to eat.
You're a cee-essing, all-around
Son of a bitch,
And I wonder, Vacerra,
How come you aren't rich.


XI. xcii

The man who calls you vicious, Zoilus, lies,
Zoilus, you're not a vicious man, but Vice.


XI. xciii

The house of Ted the poet has burned down,
And yet Apollo and the Muses frown;
Criminal negligence, their looks proclaim,
Why couldn't Ted have perished in that flame?

### XI. xcvii

Four times in one night
I know I can do,
But not once in four years,
Thelesilla, with you!

### XI. c

Flaccus, I don't want my girl to be
So skinny she can knife me with her knee,
Whose arms my rings would easily surround,
Whose spine's a saw, whose coccyx is a spear,
Nor do I want some big two-hundred-pound
Tomato; meat, not suet, I hold dear.

# From Book XII

## XII. x

This fortune hunter is a millionaire,
Yet for some reason he keeps fishing on:
Fortune, it seems, to many gives too much,
And gives enough to none.


## XII. xiii

On hatred, Auctus, rich men place reliance—
It's cheaper, far, than shelling out to clients.


## XII. xviii

Juvenal, while you're wandering around
Bothered by the noisy stir of downtown,
Or, perhaps, climbing uphill and sweating
In some smarter residential section,
While your toga flaps, or fans, around you,
Think of me, after so many winters,

Home again at Bilbilis, a farmer,
In a town that boasts of gold and iron.
Here I cultivate, with no great labor,
Platea, Boterdum (our poor natives
Name their villages with little music).
I sleep the clock around; I often idle
In my bed till halfway through the morning,
Making up for all the time I squandered
In my thirty years of active living.
Dress up? Never! I just have a servant
Sling me what I flung on a chair at bedtime.
When I do get up, the fire awaits me,
Heaped with splendid oak from the native woodlot,
And my foreman's wife has breakfast ready.
I've a huntsman, too, a fine young fellow
You'd enjoy enjoying in the copses.
Look! My foreman gives the boys a handout
Telling them to go and get their hair cut—
(If they look like men, he can work them longer).
Country living, even country dining,
Juvenal, so help me, is the finest.

## XII. xx

Your question is, why Themison
Has never married, mister?
I'll answer with another one—
Doesn't he have a sister?

## XII. xxvii

Saenia claims a mob of gangsters raped her.
This they deny; quite plausibly, I find.
Not that they all were pure and spotless virgins,
But—Saenia didn't mind.

## XII. xxx

Aper is most abstemious; so what?
A slave is praised for that, a friend is not.

### XII. xxxi

This grove, these fountains, and this arching vine
That shadows flowing water, all are mine.
So are the meadows, and the garden rose
That blooms as fair as any Paestum grows.
Herbs that are green on January ground,
An eel in his aquarium, swimming round
(He's tame, I'd have you know), pigeons as white
As the dovecote to which they come at night,
All are Marcella's gifts to me, come home
From many years of residence at Rome.
Here I am housed, a monarch, whose domain,
Small as it is, I deem the best in Spain,
And even though Nausicaa should yield
Her father's gardens, I'd prefer this field.

## XII. xxxii

Hoodoo and jinx of moving day,
Vacerra, I have seen your traps,
The remnants of what went to pay
Two years' back rent, or more, perhaps.
Your white-haired mother-in-law, your wife,
That redhead with her seven curls,
Her hunk of sister—on my life,
I never saw such dreadful girls
Except the Furies, fresh from Hell.
They trudged along in front of you,
Burnt out by thirst and cold as well,
Paler than faded boxwood's hue.
The Irus of our modern day,
You followed; people might have guessed
The Beggars' Wood was on its way
To Dunsinane, or headed west.
And what a freight! A busted cot
With one leg gone, a wooden bowl
And lantern, in a chamberpot
Taking a leak, through crack or hole.
Under a brazier, turning green
With verdigris, a flagon's neck
Stuck out; I think there must have been
A bushel, or at least a peck
Of dry saltines or salted sprat
Or desiccated tadpole spawn;

No fishpond ever stank like that,
Even with all the water gone.
There was Tolosan cheese, a wedge
Hard as a rock, a four-year-old
Chaplet of mint, turned brown as sedge,
With stringy ropes that used to hold
Garlic or onions, and the jar
Of rosin, which your mother-in-law
And dames like her employ to bar
Hair from the armpits, lips, or jaw.
Why search for housing? Why pay rent?
Trappings like these are guarantee
Of rights as permanent resident
Under the Beggars' Bridge, for free.

### XII. xl

You lie, and I believe you; you recite
Bad poems, I applaud with all my might;
You sing, I sing; you drink, and I get swacked;
You fart, and I, with due confusion, act
As as if I did it; if you want to play
Checkers, I let you beat me every day;
One thing you do alone, and I keep still.
You say I'll be remembered in your will,
Meantime, you give me nothing. Granted, I
Want nothing. Still, Pontilianus—die!

## XII. xlii

Bearded Callistratus became the bride
Of horny Afer, murmuring his vows
Like any virgin, with a veil to hide
His blushes, while the torchlight filled the house.
There was a dowry, too. All this explains
The event we are waiting for, his labor pains.

## XII. lvii

Ah, Sparsus, do you ask me why
I leave this city for the dry
Nomentum, where my fields are small
And my old shack's about to fall?
In Rome a poor man cannot find
A place to think, or peace of mind.
At dawn schoolmasters yak and clamor,
Bakers bang pans, coppersmiths hammer,
And all this din goes on all day
If not all night. Across the way
The moneychanger's killing time
By rattling every phony dime
In his tin coin box, and the sound
Competes against the thud and pound
As the gold-beaters grunt and groan
Banging their mallets on the stone.
Bellona's madmen rant and riot,

No voice, it seems, is low and quiet;
A gabby sailor, with his trunk
All bandaged up, is howling drunk,
And there's a wheedling, cadging Jew
Whining as Momma taught him to,
While, bleary-eyed, the hucksters wail,
"Sulphur for sale! Sulphur for sale!"
Perhaps a better man than I
Can count the items, specify
How many rapes my sleep endures
In this metropolis of yours.
Sparsus, you do not, cannot, sense
Such things as these; your residence
Lies in a nicer part of town,
Where even the ground-floor rooms look down
On hilltops, where your Roman field
Surpasses a Falernian yield,
And where your boundaries, far and wide,
Have ample boulevards to ride.
Your slumber's deep, your quietude
Unmarred by gabble, harsh and rude.
Light enters only at your will,
But as for me, the noisy, shrill,
Ha-ha-ing mob goes cackling by
Within three feet of where I lie.
In fact, I seem to have all Rome
Around my bed when I'm at home,
Until exhausted, sick with worry,
To my Nomentan hut I hurry.

## XII. lxi

You fear, Ligurra, that I'll write
A poem on you, out of spite,
A fierce and stinging epigram.
What makes you think I give a damn?
Your fear, or your desire, is vain:
If you've no wit, let me explain.
A Libyan lion's charge applies
To bulls, but not to butterflies.
If it's publicity you covet,
Seek out the proper agent of it,
Some poetaster (drunk), a dweller
In a dark garret or a cellar,
The kind of literary man
Whose verse is published in the can,
Or who, with chalk or charcoal, scrawls
His opuses along the walls.
You understand, I'm sure, by now;
My brand will never mark your brow.

## XII. lxxiii

I'll not believe that I'm your heir, until
I read it, after probate, in your will.

# Epilogue

IV. lxxxix

Whoa, that's enough, little volume; whoa, that's plenty!
Now we have come to the colophon, or nearly.
You still want to continue, keep on going,
You'd not be held back, even by the binding,
Just as if your business wasn't finished.
Wasn't it really finished with the preface?
Now our readers complain, are getting restive,
Even my secretary starts to mutter,
"Whoa, that's enough, little volume; whoa, that's plenty!"

# Notes

I. lv     *Fronto, bright ornament of peace and war.* Perhaps T. Catius Fronto, consul in 96 B.C. and alluded to by Pliny (*Ep.* IV.9 and VI.13) as an orator.

lxxxii     *Syene.* Ancient name of the town of Aswan, on the Nile river in Upper Egypt; the place to which Juvenal was banished.

cvii     *Vergil.* Famous Roman poet (70-19 B.C.); author of the *Bucolics, Georgics,* and the *Aeneid,* the latter a poem commemorating the travels of Aeneas and the foundation of Rome.

*Horace.* Well-known Roman poet (65-8 B.C.); author of the *Epistles, Satires, Odes,* and *Epodes.*

*Maecenas.* Roman statesman and patron of literature (d. 8 B.C.); friend and patron of both Horace and Vergil.

II. xl     *Ovid.* Roman poet (43 B.C.-17 A.D.); author of the *Metamorphoses* and *Ars Amandi* (The Art of Love).

xli     *Hecuba.* Wife of Priam, king of Troy, and mother of Paris and Hector.

*Katisha.* Elderly and ugly spinster in Gilbert and Sullivan's *Mikado;* she wished to marry the Emperor's young son.

xlviii     *baths of Nero.* Nero was Roman emperor (54-68

113

B.C.) and builder of public baths in the vicinity of the Campus Martius; he allegedly started the fire which burned Rome in 64 B.C.

*Butunti.* An insignificant little town in Calabria, Italy, near Bari.

III. xiv    *clients' dole.* A meager allowance of food. Nero substituted a dole of a hundred farthings, but Domitian restored the dinner.

xxv    *baths of Nero.* See above, II. xlvii: *baths of Nero.*

xxxv    *Phidias.* Famous Greek artist, born about 500 B.C.; he was commissioned to execute the statue of Jupiter for the temple at Olympia.

xlii    *Mentor.* Celebrated Greek artist of the fifth century B.C.; famous for his silver work, composition, and design.

xliv    *Sirens brought to mariners a happy doom.* The Sirens were virgins whom Homer described as dwelling on an island between Circe's isle and Scylla, where with their sweet song they allured and infatuated all who came by. Whoever listened to their song and drew near them never again beheld wife or child.

*Ulysses.* On his voyage home from the Trojan War, this Greek hero had to pass the Sirens. He stopped the ears of his sailors with wax and had himself bound to the mast, in order to avoid the doom of those who listened to the Sirens' song.

xlix    *Massic for you, Veian for me.* A reference to the wines of two regions. Massicus was a range of

hills on the border of Campania and Latium, in
Italy. Veii was an Italian city near Rome, be-
sieged and taken by the Romans under Camillus
in 396 B.C. The wine of Veii was of poor quality;
that of Massicus was excellent.

lvi  *Ravenna.* An Italian city on the upper Adriatic
coast.

IV. viii  *kindly Caesar.* A reference to the Emperor Domitian.

xliv  *Vesuvius.* A volcano on the Bay of Naples, in Italy.
In 79 A.D. an eruption destroyed Pompeii, Herculaneum, and Stabiae, towns located near the
mountain.

*Bacchus.* Identical with Dionysus; god of wine, and
of fertility in general. The worship of Dionysus
spread over Greece and Italy and into far Asia. In
Italy both urban and rural festivals were held
annually in the god's honor; and side by side
with public celebration, there sprang up a secret
worship—the Bacchanalia, which were associated
with so many excesses that they were put down
in 186 B.C. by decree of the Senate.

*Nysa.* A reference to the mountain where Bacchus
allegedly grew up.

*Satyrs.* Associated with Bacchus; they were ugly
woodland spirits, always fond of wine and women.

*Venus' abode.* Venus liked the slopes of Vesuvius,
perhaps because Vulcan, her husband, worked in
the heart of mountains.

*her Sparta.* As Aphrodite, Greek goddess of love, Venus was also goddess of storm and lightning, and she was represented armed at Sparta and Cythera.

*a town famous for Hercules' name.* A reference to Herculaneum.

xlvi    *haggis.* A Scottish pudding made of the internal organs of a sheep or calf.

*Picenian.* A reference to the region in Italy lying between the Adriatic Sea and the Apennines. The Picenes were a warlike, merchant people.

*Saguntum.* Town in eastern Spain, founded by the Greeks, conquered by Carthaginians, and rebuilt by Rome after 214 B.C.

*a napkin with such striped hues, As only senators may use.* This distinction belonged only to a Senator, and Sabellus was not one.

*the gardens where the golden apples used to grow.* See below, X. xciv: *Hesperides.*

lxiv    *Seven Hills.* The seven hills on which Rome was originally built: Palatine, Capitoline, Quirinal, Aventine, Caelian, Esquiline, and Viminal. The places named in this poem include many of the different regions visible from the top of the Janiculum Hill across the Tiber in Rome, and the panoramic scene of the city itself and its seven canonical hills. Today, on the place where Martial locates the villa of his friend Julius Martial, there is a large statue of Garibaldi in the center, and beside the promenade leading toward the plaza there is an inscription in travertine containing these verses from this poem of Martial:

> hinc septem dominos videre montis
> et totam licet estimare Romam
> [Whence we may see the Seven Hills,
> May estimate the scope of Rome. . . .]

The ridges of the Alban hills and of Tusculum can be seen at a distance of some fifteen miles in the southeast, Tivoli (ancient Tibur) and Palestrina (ancient Praeneste) farther off and northeastward and eastward, and the sites of Fidenae and Rubra Saxa north along the Tiber.

*Alba.* Alba Longa, a town in Latium, Italy; its foundation is traditionally ascribed to Ascanius, son of Aeneas.

*Anna Perenna.* An ancient Italian goddess, about whose exact attributes the ancients themselves were not clear; probably the moon goddess of the revolving year. About full moon on the Ides of March (then the first month of the year), in a grove of fruit trees at the first milestone on the Flaminian Way, the Romans held a feast under the open sky, wishing each other as many years of life as they drank cups of wine. This was Anna Perenna's "fruitful grove."

*Fidenae.* A town in Latium, on the Tiber river, about five miles from Rome.

*Rubrae.* Saxa Rubra, the site of a small bridgehead a few miles north of Rome.

*Mulvian Bridge.* Ancient bridge across the Tiber river north of Rome, built in 109 B.C. Later it was the site of the emperor Constantine's vision of a cross in the sky, which led him to embrace Christianity.

*Tiber.* Second longest river in Italy, rising in the Apennines and emptying into the Mediterranean about sixteen miles southwest of Rome. It was called "holy" perhaps by association with the river god: see Vergil's *Aeneid.*

*Ulysses.* Another name for Odysseus, Greek hero whose homeward voyage from the Trojan War was immortalized in Homer's *Odyssey.* The reference to his "host" was to Alcinous, king of Phaeacia, who greeted him hospitably and gave him a ship on which to complete his journey home.

*Hercules.* Son of Zeus and one of the oldest heroes in Greek mythology. Twelve tasks or labors were imposed on him through the enmity of Juno. He later aided the gods in their battle against the Giants. The reference to Hercules' "host" was to Molorchus, a shepherd who unknowingly entertained Hercules.

*Tivoli.* Town in Latium, Italy, situated on a height above the falls of the Anio river; hence the reference to Tivoli's "coolness."

*Setia.* Ancient name of Sezze, a town in Latium, Italy.

*Palestrina.* Town in Latium, Italy; ancient Praeneste.

*Julius Martialis.* A friend of Martial for thirty-three years; to judge from his cognomen, he was also born on the first of March.

V. xx   *Aqua Virgo*. One of the aqueducts by which water was brought into Rome; it was built by Agrippa in 20 B.C.

*Hermes*. Another name for Mercury, messenger of the gods. He was the escort and protector of heroes in their perilous undertakings; hence the reference to "Hermes, in whom all sons of Mars delight." He was known for inventiveness, trickery, and cunning. He was the guide of the dead and the god of sleep and dreams; perhaps these attributes account for his description as "Hermes, who wins, yet does not kill his foe." As the patron of tradespeople and thieves, he was "the ticket speculator's joy." As the slayer of Argos and patron of gymnastic skills, he was "the glory of the world of Mars . . . what gladiator equals him?" The gladiator in this poem may have adopted his *nom de guerre* as suited to his profession and his ideas of himself.

*Helius*. Roman court favorite, and prefect of Italy and Rome during the absence of Nero. At this time he had the power of life and death, even over the senatorial order. In 68 A.D. he was put to death by Nero's successor, the emperor Galba. The Helius mentioned here, however, is probably only another gladiator.

*Advolans*. Another gladiator.

xxxiv   *Hell-hound*. A reference to Cerberus, the three-headed dog who guarded the gates to Hades.

*Fronto.* Assumedly, the father of Martial.

*Flacilla.* Assumedly, the mother of Martial.

lvi    *Vergil.* See above, I. cvii: *Vergil.*

*Marcus Tullius Cicero.* Roman orator, philosopher, and statesman (106-43 B.C.); author of fifty-seven orations, books on rhetoric and oratory and philosophy, four collections of letters, and some poetry.

*Nestor.* Patriarchal leader of the Greek expedition to Troy.

*Priam.* King of Troy who was slain when the city was taken by the Greeks.

*Postumus.* A friend of Juvenal.

lxviii    *Rhone.* River in Switzerland and France.

VI. xxxv    *water clocks.* An instrument or machine to measure time by the fall or flow of a quantity of water; e.g., a clepsydra.

xlvi    *Ben Hur.* Judah Ben Hur, principal character in the novel *Ben Hur: A Tale of the Christ,* written by Lew Wallace and published in 1880.

*Blue chariot.* The chariots which contested in the Roman circuses were decked with the colors of the different factions. Of these there were originally only two, the White and the Red. At the beginning of the imperial period we hear of two more, the Green and the Blue. Two more, Gold and Purple, were introduced by Domitian but dropped out after his death. In the late Roman and Byzantine period we generally hear only of Blue and Green.

lxx     *Nestor.* See above, V. lviii: *Nestor.*
       *Priam.* See above, V. lviii: *Priam.*

VII. xix     *Argo.* The ship on which the Argonauts sailed, led by Theseus, on the quest for the Golden Fleece.

       *Clashing Rocks.* The Symplegades: in Greek mythology, two cliffs or floating islands near the entrance of the Black Sea, which crushed all vessels that tried to pass between them. The Argonauts were the first to succeed in passing through; thereafter the rocks became immovably fixed.

       *Pontic.* The Pontic sea: a reference to the Black Sea (Pontus Euxinus).

xxxi     *Chian figs.* Figs from the island of Chios, off the eastern coast of Greece.

       *Umbrian tenant.* Umbria was a region in Italy east of Etruria and west of Picenum.

       *Etruscan field.* The Etruscans were people in ancient Etruria, a region in Italy corresponding to what is now Tuscany and part of Umbria.

xxxvi     *Boreas.* The North Wind.

xlvi     *Homer.* The first and most famous Greek poet (c. 9th century B.C.); author of *Iliad* and *Odyssey.*

lxi     *your Majesty.* A reference to the Emperor Domitian (Germanicus), who in 92 A.D. forbade the erection of stalls which protruded into the streets.

xcv     *Cybele's priesthood.* Cybele, or Rhea, was mother of the Olympian gods; the Cretan Rhea became identified with the Asiatic Cybele (Great Mother). She thus symbolized the procreative power of nature, cultivation, and all other forms of social progress and civilization; and she came to be regarded as the founder of towns and cities. The priest-eunuchs of Cybele were also called the Corybantes, and the festivals of the goddess were celebrated with orgiastic frenzies. In Rome the worship of the goddess was introduced for political reasons in 204 B.C., at the command of a Sibylline oracle, and for the purpose of driving Hannibal out of Italy.

VIII. x    *Tyrian cloak.* A cloak made in Tyre, a city of Phoenicia; perhaps dyed the purple hue for which Tyre was famous. The dye had a distinct odor.

lxvii    *Corcyra's king.* A reference to Alcinous, king of Phaeacia. See above, IV. lxiv: *Ulysses.* Also XII. xxxii: *even though Nausicaa. . . .*
*Bacchus.* See above, IV. xliv: *Bacchus.*

IX. xviii    *Caesar.* The Emperor Domitian.
*Marcian flume.* The reference is to the Aqua Marcia, one of the great aqueducts which brought water to Rome. It was built by Quintus Marcius Rex in 144 B.C.
*Jove's golden rain.* Jove is identical with Jupiter. This is a reference to the "golden rain" wherein Jupiter penetrated the tower in which Danae was imprisoned, in order to seduce her.

xxxv    *Pacorus the king.* King of Parthia, Rome's greatest rival in the East.

*Parthian palace.* Parthia lay in the region which is now northeast Persia. Her kings opposed Rome.

*Dacian commander.* Dacia was a Roman province between the Carpathians and the Danube river.

*Libyan grain.* North Africa and Egypt were the granaries of Rome.

xlv *Northern Wain.* An astronomical reference to Boötes; "wain" means chariot.

*Getic skies.* The Getae probably belonged to the Thraco-Phrygian branch of the Indo-European family.

*Prometheus' crag.* Prometheus, it is said, stole fire from Olympus and gave it to man. Zeus punished him by binding him to a pillar with an eagle to consume his liver, which was nightly regenerated. Aeschylus gives the myth another form: Prometheus is punished by being chained to a rock beside the sea in the wilds of Scythia; when he refuses to divulge a secret, Zeus hurls him and the rock down into Tartarus; later he emerges into the light of day to be fastened to Mount Caucasus and torn by the eagle. In both versions of the story, Hercules finally liberates Prometheus by slaying the eagle.

*to mould this race of ours.* Another legend tells that Prometheus moulded man out of clay.

lii *Quintus.* Quintus Ovidius, Martial's friend and neighbor at Nomentum.

*April Kalends.* The first day of the second month of the year.

lxii *Tyrian dyes.* See above, VIII. x: *Tyrian cloak.*

lxviii    *Coliseum.* The amphitheater in Rome, where the circus games were held.

X. xl    *Pylades.* Nephew of Agamemnon and husband of Electra; famous for his faithful friendship with Orestes.

     *the pigs Pirithous had.* Pirithous, the friend of Theseus (as Pylades was the friend of Orestes), was rich in livestock.

xxiii    *Fifteen Olympiads gone.* That is, seventy-five years. In fact, the *lustrum* was five years, the *olympiad* four; but Martial treats them both as periods of five years.

     *Lethe.* The river of forgetfulness in Hades.

liii    *The Fates.* Greek goddesses who spun the thread of life for men at their birth: identified by the Romans with their native goddesses of fate, the Parcae. In art they appear as maidens of grave aspect: Clotho is usually represented with a spindle; Lachesis with a scroll, or a globe; and Atropos with a pair of scales or shears, or else drawing a lot.

lxii    *the Lion's sign.* The constellation Leo.

lxxxvi    *The All-Etruscan out.* The implication is that Laurus is now good for nothing at all.

xciv    *Hesperides.* The garden in which grew the golden apples which Gaea gave to Juno. Nymphs and a dragon guarded the apples.

     *King Alcinous.* King of Phaeacia, with whom Ulysses, and later Jason and Medea, find shelter

and aid. See above, IV. lxiv: *Ulysses*; see also
XII. xxxi: *even though Nausicaa....*

*Nomentan apple trees.* Nomentum was a town in
the Sabine country, about fourteen miles northeast of Rome, celebrated for its wine. Martial and
Seneca had houses here. Martial's orchard apparently produced no fruit; so he sent apples from
the city.

ciii    *Bilbilis.* The second city of Hispania Tarraconen-
sis; Martial was born there. See introduction.

*Salo.* Bilbilis (see above) stood on a rocky height
surrounded by the Salo river, a river famed for
tempering iron.

*Verona.* City in northeast Italy; a Celtic settlement
which became a Roman colony in 89 B.C.

*Catullus.* Roman lyric poet (87-54 B.C.), born in
Verona.

XI. xiii    *the Loves.* A reference to "all the Venuses and
Cupids" buried along the Flaminian Way.

*Paris.* The son of Priam of Troy, who stole Helen
from her husband Menelaus, and so brought on
the Trojan War. Here the reference is to a Roman
actor who called himself Paris.

xviii    *Diana.* Goddess of the moon; also goddess of the
hunt and protectress of wild creatures; she aided
women in childbirth.

*Calydonian boar.* Calydonia was the Roman name
for the northern part of the island of Britain.

xcii    *Zoilus.* When attacking persons, as here, Martial

always used pseudonyms to cloak his victims in anonymity. He used the true names of his friends. Zoilus was a dyspeptic literary critic of the Alexandrian period, notorious for finding fault with creative writers, especially Homer; and his name became synonymous with malignant criticism.

xciii  *Muses.* In Greek mythology, originally the nymphs of inspiring springs, then goddesses of song in general, afterward the representatives of the various kinds of poetry, arts, and sciences. Hesiod calls them the nine daughters of Zeus and Mnemosyne: Calliope, the Muse of epic song; Clio, the Muse of history; Euterpe, the Muse of lyric song; Thalia, the Muse of comedy and bucolic poetry; Melpomene, the Muse of tragedy; Terpsichore, the Muse of dancing; Erato, the Muse of erotic poetry; Polymnia, the Muse of serious sacred songs; and Urania, the Muse of astronomy.

XII. xviii  *Juvenal.* Roman satirist (47-ca. 130 A.D.).
*Bilbilis.* See above, X. ciii: *Bilbilis.*
*Platea.* A small town near Bilbilis, in Spain (perhaps named after the town in Boeotia, Greece, at the foot of Mount Cithaeron).
*Boterdum.* A small town near Bilbilis, in Spain.

xxxi  *Paestum.* A city in Lucania, Magna Graecia, Italy, originally Greek but under Roman domination after 273 B.C.

xxi  *Marcella's gifts.* Marcella was a Spanish lady whom Martial knew. See introduction.

*even though Nausicaa should yield her father's gardens.* Nausicaa was the daughter of King Alcinous of Phaeacia. "The gardens of Alcinous" were proverbial.

xxxii    *Furies.* Goddesses of vengeance; they punished without mercy all transgressions of natural order—murder, perjury, and like offenses. Euripides fixes their number at three. Later they were named: Allecto, Tisiphone, and Megaera. Aeschylus pictures them as women like Gorgons, with snakes for hair, bloodshot eyes, grinding teeth, and long black robes with blood-red girdles.

*Irus.* The beggar in the *Odyssey* who was beaten by Odysseus.

*Beggars' Wood.* Aricia's hill, where beggars took their stand.

*Dunsinane.* A reference to Shakespeare's *Macbeth,* in which "Birnam Wood shall come to Dunsinane."

*Tolosan cheese.* "Tolosan" is a Latin reference to Toulouse; i.e., cheese of Toulouse.

*Beggars' Bridge.* See above: *Beggars' Wood.*

xlii    *Bearded Callistratus became the bride of horny Afer.* "Callistratus" and "Afer" are pseudonyms. See above, XI. xcii: *Zoilus.*

lvii    *Nomentum.* See above, X. xciv: *Nomentan apple trees.*

*Falernian yield.* Falernus Ager was a fertile territory in Campania, Italy, celebrated for its wines.